JULIA DE BURGOS:
CHILD OF WATER

D0023979

Also by Carmen Rivera

La Gringa
The Loves of My Life
Trujillo: America's Dictator
La Lupe: My Life, My Destiny
Under the Mango Tree
The Next Stop
To Catch the Lightning
Betty's Garage
Water Wars
The Next Cycle
Caravan of Death
The Power of Words
A Song in the Heart
Delia's Race
Plastic Flowers

A Kiss Under The Mango Tree
Riding the Bear
Ghosts in Brooklyn
Julia (One-Act)
ameRICAN (One-Act)
Celia: The Life and Music of Celia Cruz
(co-written with Cándido Tirado)
Palladium
(co-written with Cándido Tirado)
House of Souls
(co-written with Cándido Tirado)

For more information,
www.carmenrivera-writer.com.

JULIA DE BURGOS:
CHILD OF WATER

By

CARMEN RIVERA

Red Sugarcane Press
New York

Julia de Burgos: Child of Water

June 2014. Published by Red Sugarcane Press, New York
www.redsugarcanepress.com

Copyright © 1998 Carmen Rivera

All rights reserved. No part of this publication may be reproduced, in any form or by any means, electronic, mechanical, photocopying, recording, or otherwise, without the prior written permission of the publisher.

For all performance rights including amateur and stock performances and uses of this play by educational institutions, permission must be secured from the author. Contact: Ron Gwiazda at Abrams Artists Agency, 275 Seventh Avenue, 26th floor, New York, NY 10001. ron.gwiazda@abramsartny.com

Cover Design & Book Layout by Iris Morales
Technical Advisor & eBook Designer: Adrien Bibiloni Morales

ISBN: 978-0-9884750-4-5
Library of Congress Control Number: 2014938353

Printed in the United States of America

For Cándido, always....

EPIGRAPH

In JULIA DE BURGOS: CHILD OF WATER, we have the privilege of witnessing our "Julia," as she would have like to have been perceived by all, thereby honoring her life in a truly genuine and sensitive way. Carmen Rivera not only gives us the space to discover Julia de Burgos, but also offers us the sacred space to discover the dualities within ourselves. Carmen Rivera is a great writer and a worthy ambassador of the Puerto Rican artistic community.

Brenda Torres Barreto
Puerto Rican Federal Affairs Administration
Director, New York Regional Office,
Commonwealth of Puerto Rico

Carmen Rivera's dramaturgy is an antidote for an apathetic nostalgic gaze for Puerto Rico's past. In *Child of Water,* the iconic poet Julia de Burgos is caught in an intermediary state of longing for and longing to; attempting to recreate what was, while attempting to break free and establish a new, politically engaged and self-actualized identity.

In reading this play, one becomes mesmerized by the spiritual relativity between these two women. Carmen Rivera and Julia de Burgos become symbiotic twins through their writing and desire to blur the lines between artist and creation. JULIA DE BURGOS: CHILD OF WATER positions itself as the foundation for the emerging Latina canon and Carmen Rivera as its most respected ambassador.

Jason Ramírez, Ph.D.
Author of *Carmen Rivera: Theatre of Latinidad*

CONTENTS

FOREWORD

Since her first hugely successful incursion into theatre with *La Gringa* in 1996, the longest running play in New York's Latino theatre/Off-Broadway history, every contribution Carmen Rivera has made to the canon has been important and moving. From La Lupe to Celia Cruz, Rivera has fearlessly appropriated Latina icons and made them accessible to contemporary audiences.

Now her authentic, complex portrait of the revered Puerto Rican literary/feminist/political legend, Julia de Burgos, is available to a new public, making Julia "universal," as she once said she dreamed of being.

JULIA DE BURGOS: CHILD OF WATER is an invitation into the heart and soul of the poet and patriot, the woman who would become the best known Puerto Rican poet of the century, embraced by feminists, by the Left and internationally by lovers of poetry. In CHILD OF WATER, Rivera paints a rich historical, political and cultural canvas, situating Julia in her historical moment of the 1950s; the Nationalist movement for independence from the United States; the literary fervor she shared with the iconic Pablo Neruda and the consummate story teller/politician Juan Bosch.

The play visually offers us what Julia offered us in her verses, a fierce determination to be herself, to live and die with the emblazoned banner of freedom and poetry on high. Rivera's talent lies in creating moments that define Julia's character: her authentic exchanges with her classist, sexist, racist Dominican lover, Juan Jiménez Grullón; her poignant, gut wrenching exchanges with her alter ego, the character Woman/Soul, who embodies the artist, the fighter, the champion of personal and political freedom; the exchanges with her mother where she shares her pantheistic ideals, her love, indeed her need, for nature in general, but more specifically, her river, Río Grande de Loíza; the rich and revealing interchange with Pablo Neruda where he offers advice to an angry and indignant Julia, affirming that "Art should come from love, not hate." One of the many gifts Rivera gives her audience is his response to Julia's question," What if I am surrounded by anger?" "Feel it, transform it and release it."

The conflictive dualities that de Burgos experiences provide the through line of the play. The text breathes life into the age old dilemma that women, especially artists, face: how to be a writer, have a personal life, have a career and somehow find balance. Rivera reveals the pain and beauty, the sacrifices and rewards of being an artist ("It's a curse, this longing to write … a sweet curse.") She also explores what it means to have a gift, a calling, a mission and how these talents get subverted.

Rivera gives us the gift of Julia's poetry interspersed throughout the play as a complement to the dramatic action. We experience the desperation of "Give Me My Number," the inspiration of the Latin American feminist anthem "A Julia de Burgos," which takes on another dimension as we see/hear the interaction between the Woman/Soul and Julia, and finally we experience the sadness - yet triumph - of art over death, especially in "Poem For My Death."

Just as Julia took her audiences on a journey as she wrote and recited her poems, so does Rivera take us on a journey in this play, posing implicit questions, Did Julia ever came to terms with her immense talent? Was she ever at peace with these conflicts? Was her life subsumed at the end with alcohol and escape or illness? Her body of work demonstrates that no matter what the answers, de Burgos could never escape her talent, her natural self, her mood, her times.

That is what Rivera demonstrates in this play. She captures all of this life struggle in a Polaroid as she blends Julia's words with her own words; Julia's self expression with Rivera's, Julia's rage and frustrations about the world, her work and the need to do, to write, to be, with Rivera's own…. It is a match: Julia/ Lloréns Torres, Julia/ Juan Bosch, Julia/ Pablo Neruda, Julia/ Juan Jiménez Grullón, Julia/ despair, Julia/ Carmen.

We witness the exploration and elaboration of Julia's creative process.

A cautionary tale? A love story? A model for how to be, not to be?

All of this and more in this latest incarnation of Carmen Rivera's dramatic trajectory.

So here's to our 21ˢᵗ century Julia, whose multifaceted personhood we witness at war and peace with each other throughout the play. Here's to the pure soldier of revolution and vindicator of human rights, to the dreamy Julia, to the gritty Julia, to the very human Julia, to the one the feminists embrace and to the one who loves and loses and turns her pain into art.

She is ours now thanks to Carmen Rivera and her CHILD OF WATER.

Gloria Waldman
Professor Emerita, Ph.D.
Program in Theatre at the Graduate Center and York College
City University of New York

Author of *Luis Rafael Sanchez: Pasion Teatral and* Jose (Papo) Marquez: *Vida y Obra del autor de Esquizofrenia Puertorricensis* Drama Critic, El Nuevo Día, Puerto Rico and El Diario/La Prensa

ABOUT JULIA DE BURGOS
(1914 - 1953)

JULIA DE BURGOS is one of Puerto Rico's most illustrious poets whose work has earned a place among the best Latin American and Caribbean literature of the 20th century.

Born on February 17, 1914 in Carolina, Puerto Rico, Julia Constanza Burgos García was the eldest of thirteen children. By the age of 19, she had graduated from the University of Puerto Rico with a degree in education. Shortly thereafter, she joined the Daughters of Freedom of the Puerto Rican Nationalist Party, which advocated for Puerto Rico's independence from the United States during tumultuous times of widespread poverty, major labor struggles, and political persecution. In 1940, de Burgos moved to Cuba where she associated with internationally acclaimed poets such as Cuban Nicolás Guillén and Chilean Pablo Neruda.

De Burgos published several poetry collections: *Poema en veinte surcos* (*Poem in Twenty Furrows*, 1938) and *Canción de la verdad sencilla* (*Song of the Simple Truth*, 1939). She published the books herself and promoted them in public readings and political rallies. *El mar y tú: otros poemas* (*The Sea and You*), published posthumously, included many of the poems she wrote when living in New York.

De Burgos' last years were complicated by failing health, depression, and alcoholism. She died tragically in 1953 in New York City where she was found lying on an East Harlem street unconscious and without any identification. She was buried in an unmarked grave in Potter's Field until family and friends had her exhumed and returned home to Puerto Rico on September 6, 1953, where she was received with a hero's welcome. She was 39 years old.

Julia de Burgos challenged major historical and political problems of her times: colonialism, racism, and sexism. She was a feminist and activist for national liberation at a time when it was dangerous to be either.

Publisher's Note

OPENING PRODUCTION

JULIA DE BURGOS: CHILD OF WATER opened at the Puerto Rican Traveling Theatre in New York City on May 12, 1999. It was directed by Manuel Martin; set design by Salvatore Tagliarino; lighting design by Alan Baron; costume design by Harry Nadal; choreography by Adolfo Vazquez. The original cast was as follows:

JULIA de BURGOS: Sol Miranda
WOMAN / SOUL: Lourdes Martin
JUAN ISIDRO GRULLÓN: Ricardo Puente
JUAN BOSCH & TITO ARROYO: Mateo Gómez
PABLO NERUDA, PUBLISHER, SUPER & FRIEND IN CUBA: Tony Chiroldes
MOTHER, BOSS & STRANGER: Puli Toro

CENTENNIAL PERFORMANCES

In 2014 -- the Centennial of Julia de Burgos' birth -- a conversation with the actors Amneris Morales and Belange Rodríguez resulted in a 5-City Choral reading of JULIA DE BURGOS: CHILD OF WATER. The following theatres and artists participated in honoring Julia de Burgos on February 16-17, 2014:

Teatro Círculo--New York City; Cándido Tirado, José Cheo Oliveras, Amneris Morales, Belange Rodríguez, Luis Antonio Ramos, José Antonio Melian, Renoly, Santiago, Edna Lee Figueroa, and Rubén Darío Cruz;

UrbanTheater Company--Chicago; Ivan Vega, Jasmine Cardenas, Sandra Marquez, Marilyn Camacho, Gabriel Ruiz, Ramon Camin, Edgar Sanchez, Nydia Castillo, and Mike Cherry;

Raíces Theatre--Buffalo, New York; Victoria Pérez Maggiolo, Rolando Gómez, Sheila Maldonado, Sarielys Matos, Nicholas Nieves, Ricardo Morrisroe, Mariana Cole-Rivera, Smirna Mercedes Pérez, Dewel Pérez, and Ingrid Córdova;

Bregamos Theatre--New Haven, Connecticut; Rafael Ramos; and

Corralón de San José--San Juan, Puerto Rico; Josean Ortiz, Carlos Esteban Fonseca, Jerry Segarra; Luis Enrique Romero, Rosabel Otón, Amneris Morales, and Belange Rodriguez.

1

SYNOPSIS

JULIA DE BURGOS: CHILD OF WATER is a surrealistic play that takes Julia on a journey through her own life. In much of her poetry, Julia writes about a division within herself and frequently complained about the chaos that her SOUL caused her. Her SOUL is the part of her that is the artist and the fighter that continuously confronts society's prejudices. Throughout her life, there were times that Julia wished to silence her SOUL. She was never able to come to terms with her genius.

In CHILD OF WATER, Julia throws her SOUL away and tries to live without her SOUL. The SOUL is treated as a separate character. The SOUL takes Julia back to Cuba, Washington D.C. and finally to the present, in New York City, where the SOUL and JULIA do find integration and peace. This play breaks time and space and takes place in the chasm between life and death.

SET

The set must be surrealistic and minimalist. This play occurs in a world between life and death, and the set must reflect this and NOT be grounded in a realistic way. There will be a sofa on stage left with a rocking chair next to it. A bureau is on the stage right wall and a small table (a round one that is found in a poetry café) and one chair next to it.

There is a scrim in front of the upstage wall. There should be enough room in between the wall and the scrim to have another playing area.

Lights will be very important for the play in invoking the surreal nether world that Julia de Burgos finds herself in.

CHARACTERS

1. Julia de Burgos: Puerto Rican woman – ages from 15 to 39;
2. WOMAN – Julia's Soul - ***Must NOT appear like a Soul but as a regular person***
3. Julia's mother – Puerto Rican; late 30s;
4. Juan Isidro Jiménez Grullón – Dominican; Julia's lover; very wealthy; late 30s;
5. Pablo Neruda – Chilean; poet; late 30s;
6. Juan Bosch – Dominican; writer in exile in Cuba; early 40s;
7. Grullón's friend – Cuban – late 20s;
8. Boss;
9. Publisher;
10. Super;
11. Tito Arroyo – Puerto Rican; poet; early 40s.
12. Voice-Over - Julia's voice in the infinite

*Please note if voice-overs can not be recorded; they may be performed by the Soul.

Dramaturg: Cándido Tirado
English translation of poetry: Susana Cabañas
Additional translation: Carmen Rivera

ACT 1

SCENE 1: A Street in East Harlem -- July 1953

SCENE 2: Apartment, NYC -- 1953

SCENE 3: Apartment, NYC -- 1953

SCENE 4: A river in Puerto Rico -- 1929

SCENE 5: La Havana, Cuba -- 1941

SCENE 6: La Havana, Cuba -- 1941

SCENE 7: Juan Bosch's house, Cuba -- 1941

SCENE 8: Apartment, La Havana, Cuba -- 1941

SCENE 9: La Havana, Cuba -- 1942

ACT 2

SCENE 1: A Coffee House, NYC -- 1949

SCENE 2: Apartment, Washington D.C. -- Mid 1940s

SCENE 3: Apartment, Washington D.C. -- Mid 1940s

SCENE 4: Poetry Cafes, Washington D.C. -- Mid 1940s

SCENE 5: Apartment, NYC -- 1953

SCENE 6: Apartment, NYC -- Early 1950s

SCENE 7: Goldwater Hospital -- 1953

SCENE 8: Goldwater Hospital -- 1953

SCENE 9: Río Grande de Loíza -- 1953

ACT I

PLACE: A Street in East Harlem
TIME: July 1953

> *Lights rise softly to reveal a forest in the shadows
> reflected on the scrim upstage. Coquies are heard as
> well as the sound of a river flowing. In this dim lighting
> a voice is heard. It is Julia's.*

VOICE-OVER: "I was a strong outburst of the forest and river
and, as a voice between two echoes, I climbed the hills. From
one side the water's hands stretched towards me, and the
mountain's roots took hold of me from the other. From there my
voice of the present, bare of language, spreads over the world
as it came from the earth!!"

> *A Woman enters. She is having a difficult time walking.
> She is stumbling and periodically stops to catch her
> breath. She is gasping for air and is dressed in a
> hospital gown with a worn coat on. She is also
> coughing a great deal. This is JULIA DE BURGOS.*

JULIA: They think they can keep me locked up...

> *Julia checks behind her.*

They can't do that...they don't know who I am!

> *She stumbles and falls and starts coughing.*

I'm not going back...Okay, I have to get to...

> *Julia starts coughing again.*

...uhhh – it's hurts...

> *She holds her chest. She looks behind her again.*

I hope they're gone. Leave me alone! I'm not going back!

7

She turns around and appears to be yelling at someone.

JULIA: Okay, where…this way…yeah…no…okay, I know I'm close…

Julia stops and looks around her. She walks in the opposite direction.

No, it's this way – It has to be, because it wasn't the other way. I was there so many times; how come I can't find it? Where is the river? I know it's here…somewhere…I can feel it…I can smell it… WHERE IS THE RIVER?!

She starts crying and coughing again.

I know it's this way.

She continues walking and begins coughing again and falls on her knees.

Okay, just hold on Julia just a little while, keep walking Julia, don't give up….walk Julia walk….Dammit, Julia, why can't you remember?… "Am I the roving bridge between the dream and death? Present…! From what side of the world do they call me, from what front? I am at high sea…In the middle of time… Who will win? Present! Am I alive? Am I dead? Present! Here! Present…!"

JULIA begins to cough a lot and cannot catch her breath. She tries to walk like this. After a few beats she collapses. Another WOMAN enters. She finds Julia. She goes over to Julia and checks her temperature, as lights fade.

VOICE-OVER: "I was the quietest one. A voice almost without echo. A conscience spread in syllables of anguish scattered and tender, through all the silences."

END OF SCENE 1.

SCENE 2
PLACE: An Apartment, NYC

> *Lights up on entire stage. The WOMAN is holding
> JULIA. Julia is barely conscious. The WOMAN lays
> her down; she is desperate and angry.*

WOMAN: Julia, wake up, come on wake up! After all this time
– I finally found you. Wake up!!! Julia, Julia, wake up!

> *The WOMAN shakes JULIA.*

Wake up!! You're not getting off this easy! You have no right –
come on, let's go…you're gonna fight whether you like it or
not!!

> *The WOMAN forces JULIA on her feet and makes her
> walk. JULIA is NOT completely unconscious now –
> she's groggy and is mumbling incoherently.*

Let's go; let's go; walk…

> *JULIA cannot stand on her own.*

Do you know how long it took for me to find you? I couldn't
find you, and I looked and looked – WALK!!! Every time I got
close, and I thought I would find you – you disappeared. Julia –
come on try to walk.

> *JULIA starts to come to a little. Her speech is muffled.*

JULIA: I don't want to go back to the hospital.

> *She barely gets these words out.*

WOMAN: You have to walk Julia.

JULIA: Let me go!…please…

> *JULIA becomes frantic.*

JULIA: NO! Don't take me back.

JULIA starts coughing violently. She lays down on the sofa and finally passes out. There is a short pause as the WOMAN looks at JULIA.

WOMAN: "You go on being a poem, Julia de Burgos; the one that has nothing of a bourgeois, the one who sings without a harp in the gardens and curls even your soul with a storm…"

END OF SCENE 2.

SCENE 3:
PLACE: The Apartment, NYC

JULIA is sleeping. The WOMAN takes out a music box from the drawer. She opens it and music plays. She takes a poem out of the music box and reads it. JULIA starts to groan. The WOMAN puts the music box away.

WOMAN: Julia.

Julia moans. She's in pain and still has difficulty breathing.

JULIA: I need water.

WOMAN: Okay.

JULIA: Nurse, nurse...

WOMAN: Sit up slowly.

JULIA does so. She's very groggy and cannot walk on her own. The WOMAN gets a glass of water and JULIA drinks it.

JULIA: You're not the nurse.

WOMAN: I know.

JULIA takes a closer look at the Woman.

JULIA: Oh my god…

She starts coughing again. The WOMAN helps JULIA sit down on the sofa.

JULIA: …I thought I'd never see you again.

WOMAN: Me too…

JULIA: I want you to get out of here!

WOMAN: NO, I'm not leaving you!

JULIA gets up and tries to push the WOMAN, but she loses her footing and falls into the WOMAN.

WOMAN: Easy, easy…

The WOMAN puts Julia down on the sofa. Julia continues coughing.

JULIA: How did you find me?

WOMAN: You…

JULIA: Me?

WOMAN: You…even though you thought you killed me, you wished me here and I came.

JULIA: I did not…

WOMAN: I heard you…the river heard you…

JULIA: Spirits live in the river.

WOMAN: Now I am here.

JULIA: I want you to go.

WOMAN: You need me.

JULIA: I don't need you. I never needed you.

WOMAN: I saved you.

JULIA: You saved me?

WOMAN: I found you on the street. I brought you here.

JULIA: Thank you for helping, you can leave now.

WOMAN: I'm not leaving you like this.

JULIA: Like what?

WOMAN: Like this! Look at you! You look horrible.

JULIA: You don't look so good either…I need a drink. Why don't we have a toast to how great we look!!

> *JULIA stumbles around the room – she's looking for a bottle of liquor.*

JULIA: I thought I had…Where?…

WOMAN: Didn't you get clean in the hospital?

> *JULIA looks underneath sofa.*

JULIA: I thought there was a bottle here…. I don't remember where….

WOMAN: Why do you poison yourself?

JULIA: Because I want to.

WOMAN: I threw them out.

JULIA: What?

WOMAN: I threw out all the bottles.

> *JULIA starts laughing.*

JULIA: Thank God you're here to rescue me.

WOMAN: You need to get a hold of yourself.

JULIA panics and frantically searches the apartment...
she looks underneath the table...in the drawers.

JULIA: There's no way you could know where they all were.

WOMAN: Would you sit down!

JULIA: Impossible.

WOMAN: I found them all.

JULIA: I hate you.

WOMAN: You can't hate me; I am part of you. I am YOU!

JULIA: Then I hate me.

WOMAN: You don't mean that.

JULIA: YES I do!

The WOMAN gets very angry.

WOMAN: I am a part of your life, and I was part of you before you were born...I will always be a part of you. It is not possible for us to separate – No matter how hard you try you can not tear us apart – I am your soul! You tried to throw me away, but I am still connected to you...I felt your thoughts – I still feel your thoughts. I felt you dream of the river.

JULIA: I was looking for the bar where my friends are...Oh I remember...

JULIA goes to her coat pocket and takes out a liquor
bottle.

You didn't know where every bottle was.

JULIA takes a drink. There isn't much liquor left.

If it was good for papi – it's good enough for me!

JULIA takes another drink.

You're not going to stop me?

WOMAN: No.

JULIA: Do you want some?

WOMAN: No.

JULIA: There isn't that much anyway. Am I worth saving now?

The WOMAN doesn't answer.

JULIA: No answer...so NO...I'm not worth saving.

WOMAN: Of course you are.

JULIA: Then save me...let's go, come on...SAVE Julia de Burgos...she needs so much saving...UH, what are you waiting for!!

Pause.

JULIA: Get out of here!

The WOMAN doesn't move.

JULIA: I threw you out before, and I'll throw you out again.

The WOMAN stands up.

WOMAN: "Almost human, the screams of the night left. She lifted me all at once with her starry hand."

This poem surprises JULIA.

JULIA: SHUT UP!

WOMAN: I know you want me to stay.

JULIA: Wrong!

WOMAN: You brought me back.

JULIA: No, I didn't.

WOMAN: You're not happy, I know you dream of going back to Puerto Rico....

JULIA: Wrong again! You're not as smart as you think you are! You don't know what I'm thinking.

WOMAN: Yes I do AND you miss mami.

> *JULIA takes another drink.*

JULIA: Shut up!

WOMAN: I miss her too!

JULIA: I said shut up!

WOMAN: If she were here, our life would have been so different.

JULIA: Don't you dare talk about mami!!!

WOMAN: "She never forgot your eyes of a lost dove when, with me in her arms, she lingered in the grasses...."

JULIA: Please...stop....

END OF SCENE 3.

SCENE 4:
PLACE: A River in Puerto Rico
TIME: 1929

> *JULIA goes to attack the WOMAN when ...the lights on the stage fade a bit, and the lights behind the scrim illuminate very dream-like. JULIA walks in front of the scrim. A Woman appears from behind the scrim....It is JULIA'S MOTHER. The sound of a river is heard. The WOMAN walks behind the scrim.*

MOTHER: Here you are. I knew I'd find you here.

JULIA: Mami?

MOTHER: You've been gone for hours. I was looking for you all evening. It's not good for you to be out at night.

JULIA: Mami…it's you?

MOTHER: Your father is worried about you.

JULIA: Worried?!

MOTHER: Yes, he didn't know where you were; I knew you were at the river.

JULIA: Worried?! He's always angry at me.

MOTHER: You should come back home now; he's not at home; he left for the night.

JULIA: I wish he would leave forever.

MOTHER: Don't say that Julia; he's your father!…It's too late to be here by the river.

JULIA: I just want to stay a little longer.

MOTHER: It's a long walk up the mountain, back to the house, and it's getting dark.

JULIA: Why does he have to fight all the time?

MOTHER: That's how he is…he's also very angry that you missed some days of school last week.

JULIA: I am going to school.

MOTHER: We're getting letters from the principal.

JULIA: Mami you know I love school, it's just everything is easy – my grades are good… so… so… I… sometimes I leave.

MOTHER: You almost got arrested today.

JULIA: But I didn't.

MOTHER: You were lucky.

JULIA: It's MY right to put MY flag anywhere I want on MY island.

MOTHER: You cannot put the Puerto Rican flag on the Columbus Statue in San Juan – in front of all the military offices AND you can not leave school to do that…. I don't EVER want to find out that you've a committed a crime!

JULIA: My flag is NOT a crime?!

MOTHER: You cannot fight an entire army – you are a young girl, and they do horrible things to Nacionalistas.

JULIA: Mami, they're doing horrible things to Puerto Rico.

MOTHER: Julia, no more of these crazy things….Julia, Julia answer me.

JULIA: Okay…for now – when I'm a grown-up I can do whatever I want.

MOTHER: It is important to get an education and you're smart…you're almost finished with high school. Your father wants you to go to college.

JULIA: Of course I want to go to college, but he wants me to get an education for the wrong reason.

MOTHER: It doesn't matter what you do with your education – as long as you get it.

JULIA: Papi wants me to work for the Americans.

MOTHER: He just wants you to have a good job.

JULIA: The Americans were the ones who took his job in the tobacco fields. And he believes in annexation. How could he?

We should all be fighting the military. – If we all fought we could win.

MOTHER: Mama, when you do grow up you will see that not everything is possible…that's life.

JULIA: But if we don't try, if we don't fight back, we'll never know.

MOTHER: Fighting with your father is not going to free Puerto Rico.

JULIA: At least you admit we're not free….

MOTHER: Ah Julita, you can't be that sensitive…

JULIA: Mami, when something is wrong, it's wrong!…

   Pause.

Why do you let papi hit you?

MOTHER: When you grow…

JULIA: Stop telling me when I grow up I will understand …If growing up means I will understand papi's abuse OR the American occupation and all the other bad things that happen in this world - then I don't want to grow up!! I don't want to understand that. There's nothing to understand. It's ALL wrong!

MOTHER: Julia, I don't know why all these things happen, but they do, and we do the best we can. It's not easy to change the way things are.

JULIA: Yes it is – it's so easy. The Americans can just pick up and leave - Papi doesn't have to hit you – he doesn't have to drink – he just stops and that's it. Doesn't he understand how much pain he causes – how can he say he loves you and then hit you? When he doesn't drink he's happy and he reads us stories and we ride horses or we go…swimming in the river or even take care of the farm - everything is great…Doesn't he see the difference? – all of us do…Don't you see the difference mami?

Or is that something else that I'll understand when I'm grown-up?

MOTHER: Ay mama, I don't know...But you're almost an adult now.

JULIA: And I don't understand anything. I wish we could all live in your castle in the river.

MOTHER: Only spirits can live there.

JULIA: I wish I was a spirit then.

MOTHER: We all have spirit inside of us. Look another spirit passed through the river.

JULIA: Where do you think it's going?

MOTHER: To the world - they keep the waters flowing all around the world, and the river keeps us all connected to each other...we can never be alone - they can even take us to God.

JULIA: Do you think God knows about what's happening down here?

MOTHER: Of course he does.

JULIA: Why doesn't he do something?

MOTHER: I CAN'T answer ALL your questions Julia ...It's late mama...

> *Mother exits. Lights shift. JULIA is sitting down stage center.*

JULIA: Mami, Mami...Mami I love you.

WOMAN: She loved us.

JULIA: You drove her crazy...you got me in trouble all the time.

WOMAN: She always loved you.

JULIA: Mami was always there for me...she never judged me or said I was crazy no matter what– she loved all of her children. I still miss her so much. She was the only one who really loved me.

WOMAN: That's not true.

JULIA: Yes it is.

WOMAN: Your sister Consuelo loved you.

JULIA: Okay, one more person…

WOMAN: I love you...Many people love your poetry…

JULIA: But they didn't know me.

WOMAN: You are in your work.

JULIA: Mami never heard most of it.

WOMAN: I think she did.

> *The WOMAN remains behind the scrim. The lights shift to illuminate the downstage area, which is the river. JULIA approaches the river, this time with a suitcase and a book. TIME – 1939.*

JULIA: Mami, mami, I can't believe you've been gone for only several months. I still hear your voice; smell your perfume; I can't fix my hair the way you used to…I'm sorry I haven't visited you for two weeks – I've been busy in San Juan. A lot has happened. Look mami, my second book – SONG OF THE SIMPLE TRUTH. I won a prize for it. People in San Juan think I'm pretty good…. I can't believe that I've been meeting all these amazing artists: the Chilean poet Gabriela Mistral and Luis Palés Matos and Clemente Soto Vélez, Juan Antonio Corretjer and Luis Lloréns Torres. Can you believe it? A little country girl from the mountains in the same company as Palés Matos. Luis Lloréns Torres – he became my mentor. This is almost too good to be true. Our national poet is going to help me…I am spending a lot of time with all these great artists – we drink coffee, talk about politics, poetry, philosophy…

The MOTHER appears behind the scrim and looks lovingly at JULIA.

JULIA: ...oh - there's going to be another war in Europe – things aren't getting better in the world – ANYWAY um...you might not like this – but we are all Nationalists too – we dedicate our writing to the cause of Puerto Rican Liberation – I even got a promotion in the Nationalist Party. I'm the secretary of the party, the whole party. I get to work directly with Don Pedro Albizu Campos, our great leader ...That's not the only news I have...God I miss you mami...I have something very important to tell you – Um...Don't be worried, but I'm going to New York City. A lot of strange things are happening in Puerto Rico now, the massacres in Rio Piedras and Ponce...Don Albizu was arrested and seven other Nationalists...it's a little dangerous now, so I think I should leave - for a little while anyway. But don't be concerned for me, really, I won't be alone, I met a wonderful man. He's a doctor from the Dominican Republic, Juan Isidro Grullón; He's smart and charming. He's a Socialist – committed to the struggle for a better world. I know you say things don't change, BUT I have faith they can. So does Juan. He also says he loves me a lot. We could do a lot of work in New York City...The Nationalist movement is very strong there and I can meet many more artists – and I'll have a bigger audience for my poetry AND Manhattan is also an island - it has two rivers ... this is not really a goodbye - more like I'll see you soon. I'm a little scared, but I know it's the right thing to do. So I'm certain that I'll find you there. This is for you mami.

JULIA THROWS HER BOOK INTO THE RIVER. A car horn is heard.

JULIA: That's Juan. I'll see you in New York. Meet me at the river mami...

JULIA takes one last look.

JULIA: Bendición...

MOTHER takes the book JULIA left for her. There is shift in lights. JULIA remains down stage, center. The WOMAN comes from behind the scrim.

JULIA: I miss mami.

WOMAN: Me too.

JULIA starts laughing.

WOMAN: What?

JULIA: I'm just remembering…you hated when Lloréns gave you criticism.

WOMAN: He was wrong.

They laugh together.

JULIA: He was a great friend. I saw him frequently in New York. He helped me with jobs…he was always generous. I was with him when he died.

> *JULIA tries to get up; she's sick again. She's stiff and has difficulty walking. The WOMAN helps JULIA to the sofa. JULIA lies down, and the WOMAN puts a blanket over her.*

JULIA: I should have never left Puerto Rico…

WOMAN: It's so easy for you to say that now. What if someone had tried to stop you?

JULIA: I wish someone had.

WOMAN: God help the person that stood in your way.

JULIA: God help the person that stood in YOUR way…I abandoned everything I knew to chase empty dreams.

WOMAN: They weren't empty. Julia, remember – You were so full of life and excitement; you were going to change the world – you were going to free the oppressed, feed the hungry – protest injustice all over the world - win a Nobel Prize for Literature…

JULIA: Those weren't my dreams.

WOMAN: We had them together.

JULIA: Leaving Puerto Rico was the biggest mistake of my life…I hated what you did to me.

WOMAN: I went along with you Julia! I let your heart take me everywhere it wanted to go. I never stood in your way.

JULIA: You kept me from love with your great "poetry" dreams!

WOMAN: I believed in your love…I fought for your love… when you loved somebody, you really loved them–even if it was a squirrel or a little coqui or a bird…or a person.

JULIA: Everyone I ever loved is gone.

WOMAN: You loved others more than you loved yourself.

  Pause.

JULIA: I really thought he loved me.

WOMAN: I believe he did too…but he wasn't strong enough for you.

END OF SCENE 4.

SCENE 5:
PLACE: Apartment – La Havana, Cuba
TIME: 1941

> *Light shift to reflect the sunrise. The WOMAN exits behind the scrim. JUAN ISIDRO JIMÉNEZ GRULLÓN comes from behind the scrim. JULIA rises to greet him. They kiss tenderly. He removes her dress – revealing a slip then he takes off his shirt. JULIA'S hair is loose. Soft music plays. She brings him downstage into the apartment. They kiss again. As they begin to make love, there will be a choreographed dance.*

JULIA: "I want to give myself to you.

Completely…
And, with passion, empty my sighs in your soul
thirsty of sorrow
and teach you to suffer
and see in your serene eyes the black tears
that the pain of living has brought to my doors
Then…
You will know the mystery
That my sad eyes enclose;
And you will know that life is not a dream
Where you have bathed
your short existence in the world.
Then…
You will fill the void that your soul harbors
with the sweet vibration of my sorrow
replete with calm;
and you will know, once in your life
that pain is the sublime sanctuary of the soul
I would like to empty the flower of my sorrow
in your soul and give myself to you
Completely…"

They lay on the floor under a blanket. JUAN is sleeping lightly. JULIA gets up and follows a sunrise. The lights start to illuminate as the sun rises. JUAN rolls over and realizes that JULIA is not there.

JUAN: Julia?

JULIA: Here.

JUAN: What are you doing?

JULIA: The sun is rising.

JUAN: Hm…

JULIA: The rays are sliding through the window. It's beautiful, come look.

JUAN gets up - with a sheet wrapped around him - and joins her. He hugs her and encloses her in the sheet.

JULIA: Isn't it beautiful?

JUAN: You're beautiful.

JULIA: This is the most special time of day. It's a birth.

JUAN: I'm glad you joined me here.

JULIA: I love Cuba...I love it much more than New York City. It was cold, flat and gray...I can't believe people live there. It's like one big concrete, impersonal jail...

JUAN: You did very well for yourself in New York. We were only there six months and you made your mark...JULIA DE BURGOS – POET...La Prensa interviewed you. I can't believe how quickly success happened for you. And that group of writers gave you a tribute.

JULIA: Which you didn't go to...hm, hm, hm...

JUAN: I had to work, someone has to support the big shot poet from Puerto Rico.

JULIA: I didn't need your help, like you said, I did well for myself. But Cuba is different. First of all it's warm...I'm so inspired here...My mind can't stop thinking and creating. The poetry is just flowing.

JUAN: You seem to be writing a lot.

JUAN pulls away from her.

JULIA: There are so many things to do in Cuba...when you go to a poetry reading the place is overflowing with people, but you don't know that because you haven't come to any of my poetry readings here either. I can't believe you. You better start attending the readings...

JUAN: Or what?

Playfully.

JULIA: Or I might have to beat you up.

They kiss.

JUAN: I love you.

JULIA: I love you too…This is the right place for us. The people I've met at La Universidad de la Habana are very progressive. You know my professor got me a job writing articles for the newspaper ORIENTE. I start next week. And I'm so happy in my classes, the science and literature and Latin.

JUAN: Latin?! Another language? That makes 10 or 15 languages, right?

JULIA: Don't be funny, just Latin, Greek and French…this way I can read Aristotle and Dante in their original languages… Once I know Greek I hear it's easy to learn Russian. I also want to study German so I can read Kant or Zweig.

JUAN: When are you going to have time for me?

JULIA: Don't be a baby! I can whisper to you loving things in Latin. Es homo pulcherrimus.

> *After she whispers something in Latin to JUAN, she tickles him.*

JUAN: Stop! Stop! STOP!

JULIA: I'm just playing.

JUAN: I don't like to play like that.

JULIA: Sorry.

> *JUAN gets up.*

JULIA: Where are you going?

JUAN: I have to do some things.

JULIA: What's the matter with you? We were having such a good time.

JUAN: All you've done all morning is talk about yourself. I feel like I'm living in Cuba all alone.

JULIA: That's not my fault. You don't want to do anything with me.

JUAN: You don't want to do anything I want to do.

JULIA: What do you want to do? You're not even going to the political meetings with me…you're a socialist and you're not doing anything about it. Juan, there's another war in the world – there's a lot to be done.

JUAN: I'm aware of that.

JULIA: Well?

JUAN: I don't want to fight with you.

JULIA: I don't want to fight either.

JUAN: We'll talk about it when I get back okay.

JULIA: I want to talk about it now.

JUAN: I have to take care of something.

JULIA: I'll go with you.

JUAN: NO, no – you stay here.

JULIA: No I want to go out with you. You just said we don't do anything together. Maybe we can get something to eat...

JUAN: Julia, no…

JULIA: Juan…

JUAN: Okay get dressed.

They get dressed.

JUAN: You know I do love you.

JULIA: I love you too.

They hug – but it is awkward. The lights shift. They are downstage. A male friend approaches JUAN.

FRIEND: Juan?

JUAN: *(Juan is very uncomfortable.)* Hi. How are you?

FRIEND: I'm fine. What's new?

JUAN: Not much.

There is an awkward pause.

JULIA: Hello, I'm Julia de Burgos.

FRIEND: Hello.

JUAN: She's a friend of mine ...who I met at the university.

JULIA: What?

FRIEND: *(to Julia)* Great, what are you studying?

JUAN: Good to see you. We have to go.

FRIEND: Okay. Take care. Let's get together.

JUAN: Sure.

FRIEND: Hasta luego.

JUAN: Bye.

JULIA: Goodbye, Juan's friend!

JUAN: Would you stop it?

JUAN drags JULIA in the opposite direction. Friend exits.

JULIA: You're very rude – you didn't even introduce me to your friend.

JUAN: I knew you were going to start a fight.

JULIA: A friend…a friend, A FRIEND…I'm a friend you met at the university?! You've never even been to the university.

JUAN: Julia forget about it?!

JULIA: How dare you?

JUAN: You don't understand.

JULIA: UNDERSTAND?! You told that friend of yours – who ever he is - that I was your friend. You just denied that I exist in your life. What is there to understand about that?

JUAN: He knows my family.

JULIA: So? Juan why shouldn't your family know that we're together?…Juan?

JUAN: I told them we weren't together anymore.

JULIA: I can't believe this is happening. I left Puerto Rico and then I went to New York with you and now Cuba....

JUAN: I had to Julia. I swear I had no choice.

> *JULIA walks away from him. JUAN chases and grabs her.*

JUAN: They made me.

JULIA: Don't touch me!

JUAN: Julia, they said they would cut off my money.

JULIA: So let them cut you off. You make a lot of money at the pharmaceutical company.

JUAN: It's not the same thing. My family is so difficult.

JULIA: I don't want to know anything about your family. You're not the man I thought you were. You don't even love me, do you?

JUAN: Julia I love you.

JULIA: No you don't…at least be a man and say what you feel!

JUAN: I do love you.

JULIA: Say the truth! I'm not good enough for your family. Say it!

JUAN: You're making this worse.

JULIA: Say it, Julia you're not good enough for my family; you're not good enough for me.

JUAN: I'm not like my family.

JULIA: Did you ever plan to tell them we're practically man and wife?...Oh…Julia is not good enough…

JUAN: God you fight like a man – you don't shut up!!

JULIA: You're such a hypocrite!

JUAN: Julia you're making a scene.

JULIA: …She's too poor, a poor Puerto Rican girl from the mountains….what kind of Socialist are you? Let me tell you – a Champagne Socialist!!

JUAN: Julia shut up!

JULIA: When it comes to living your philosophy, Socialism goes out the window.

JUAN: Julia ya!

JULIA: Don't you dare tell me YA!!!

She pushes him away.

Get away from me – get away…

JUAN exits. As the WOMAN says the following poem, JULIA writes it down.

WOMAN: "I, a fatalist,
   I, inside myself,
   always waiting for something
   that my mind can't define.
   I, multiple, as in a contradiction,
   I, universal, drinking life
   in each shooting star,
   in each sterile scream,
   in each sentiment without borders.
   And all for what?
   To go on being the same."

END OF SCENE 5.

SCENE 6
PLACE: Apartment - La Havana, Cuba

LIGHTS shift. JULIA walks to the bureau. She takes out the music box. JULIA HUMS the melody from the box. THIS IS THE SAME MUSIC BOX THAT THE WOMAN OPENED AT THE BEGINNING OF THE PLAY. Julia takes out a string of pearls and puts it on.

JULIA: Juan are you ready?

Julia calls out to him. She puts on earrings while she's waiting.

Juan, come on I don't want to be late.

Juan enters. He is in pajamas.

JULIA: You're not dressed.

JUAN: I'm not going.

JULIA: You promised me you would go.

JUAN: I changed my mind.

JULIA: You can't do that.

JUAN: They invited you, not me.

JULIA: Oh come on Juan, don't be immature.

JUAN: I don't feel like spending time with artists and listening to them talk about what's wrong with the world…and how they know how to fix it. It gets boring.

JULIA: Juan Bosch is one of the greatest writers from your country, and he had to leave the Dominican Republic because of Trujillo's dictatorship, and he's boring? Maybe you're boring.

JUAN: Everything's a fight with you.

JULIA: I'm not fighting. I don't understand you…You should be enthusiastic about being invited to his house.

JUAN: I'm not going, that's it.

JULIA: I'm going to Juan Bosch's house. Would you get dressed?

JUAN: I said I wasn't going. You can't force me – just like I can't force you to do anything you don't want to do.

JULIA: Fine. See you later.

> *JULIA exits apartment. JUAN retreats behind the scrim.*

END OF SCENE 6.

SCENE 7
PLACE: Juan Bosch's house -- La Havana, Cuba

> *Lights Shift. JUAN BOSCH and PABLO NERUDA enter.*

PABLO: Bosch, she's amazing.

BOSCH: Didn't I tell you that?

PABLO: She sees; she hears something totally different than the rest of us.

BOSCH: The first time I heard her read poetry, I felt like a train hit me. She was simple, direct and powerful.

PABLO: She reads with so much emotion – the poetry just flows out of her, you don't know it's a poem until she's half way through it. I don't think she even understands her talent.

BOSCH: Those are the best artists.

PABLO: She's the chosen one – she's been called to be the voice of Latin America.

JULIA enters.

JULIA: Juan, the view from your terrace is so beautiful.

BOSCH: Thank you.

JULIA: The sounds of the waves are so peaceful and the moonlight...ah...I felt my skin burning in the moonlight. Despite all the tragedy in the world, being immersed in nature assures me that somehow, somewhere God exists.

BOSCH: Sorry to disappoint you; God doesn't exist.

PABLO: Be careful Bosch; God is in people's lives whether you like it or not.

BOSCH: I'm sure the communist party would like to know that Pablo Neruda believes in God.

PABLO: I didn't say I believe in God; I said God is important in people's lives or rather the idea of God.

JULIA: I'm not sure what God means – but there's definitely...some force out there. I am certain it is not a misogynistic, patriarchal God that delights in punishing people.

BOSCH: Now you're talking about the church – It is one thing to have corrupt government oppress its own citizens, but it is another thing when the church supports those governments. The last concern for the church is the people they serve.

PABLO: I don't know why you are surprised by that Juan…the church has always been complicit with governments and armies and rich feudal families…that is the oldest alliance in the world.

JULIA: That's what happening in Puerto Rico – the government, the United States army and "The Church" – they've all conspired against el pueblo Puertorriqueño. Nobody is fighting for the people…no one knows who to trust. Half the island supports the United States – we're colonized, we're divided – we're scared. That's unbelievable to me.

BOSCH: What does the church do?

JULIA: Nothing.

BOSCH: Doesn't that make you furious?

JULIA: Of course it does! I'm trying to do what I can…join organizations, write poems that document the oppression.

BOSCH: We need to take a stand against the church. That's the only way the world can be a better place.

PABLO: We're writers Juan…we can take our stands with the only weapons we have – our thoughts, our stories, our feelings, our ideas, our pens…that's as powerful as any army…that's why you're here living in exile – that's why we're all living in exile.

BOSCH: That's not the point. I'm aware of what our weapons are. I repeat, WE need to take an ACTIVE stand against the church – more people have been killed in the name of God than any other entity known to humanity.

JULIA: But you cannot blame God – God is not the church

PABLO: My point!

BOSCH: People's belief in God created the church.

JULIA: No, powerful men, who want to own real estate and have political office created the church.

PABLO: I agree with Julia. God has nothing to do with the church.

BOSCH: You should know better Pablo...I'm disappointed in you.

PABLO: Being a communist doesn't mean you DON'T have faith!

JULIA: I agree with you. *(to Pablo)*

BOSCH: Julia, you can not listen to Pablo...he feels nostalgic for Chile...I'm surprised nostalgia has softened you.

PABLO: Of course, I miss Chile...desperately, as I am sure you miss Santo Domingo and Julia misses Puerto Rico...But one has to have faith Juan.

BOSCH: I have faith; I have faith that we will have revolutions all over the world.

PABLO: Do you have faith in the spirit?

BOSCH: Don't tell me you do.

PABLO: I do. I pray often.

BOSCH: In a church?

PABLO: Sometimes, when there's nobody in it.

BOSCH: You don't want anyone to see you?

PABLO: I like the quiet. My prayers are clearer.

JULIA: I used to do that when I was at the university. It was so peaceful...*(reflective)*. But now I even wonder if God hears prayers anymore.

PABLO: Faith, Julia.

JULIA: Look at the world Pablo...there's too much unhappiness. Look how Spain was destroyed by Civil War, and now the war in Europe...how many people have died...so many people are starving, suffering and nobody cares. It breaks my heart. God's not listening.

BOSCH: So you don't have faith?

JULIA: I do, but faith in humanity and what WE can do.

BOSCH: I can live with that.

JULIA: I agree with you too Juan, to a certain extent – I don't think we should tell people not to believe in God...people are not going to stop believing in God because one person tells them NOT to...and I do believe in faith. I am a Pantheist – I believe in the immense power of nature - and we can tap into that power to change our life.

VOICE – OFF-STAGE: Sr. Bosch, telephone.

BOSCH: Excuse me for just a second. I'm expecting an important call from Santo Domingo. I have certain friends that oblige me with news from home.

JUAN BOSCH gets up and exits.

JULIA: I just want to tell you that I love your work...I memorized your *TWENTY POEMS OF LOVE* when I was a teenager.

PABLO: Thank you. Once your work is published and disseminated you never know who's going to be affected by it. I saw you read a poem last week. It was good.

JULIA: You saw me?

PABLO: At the university.

JULIA: Oh no – I read some new work – it was so rough.

PABLO: I was impressed with the one that began with Ay, ay, ay, mi grifa negra...I think that's it.

JULIA: "Ay, ay that I am grifa and pure black; kinkiness in my hair, kafir in my lips; and my flat nose Mozambique…" Then it goes….wait – I can't remember all of it – I'm just memorizing it now…ah yes…"Ay, Ay, Ay, my black race flees and with the white runs to become brown; to become the race of the future, fraternity of America!"

PABLO: It's very powerful – it stayed with me all night, but if I may…I have a comment.

JULIA: Of course I'll take criticism from Pablo Neruda.

PABLO: It's not criticism, but you read the poem with too much anger – the other night.

JULIA: Too much anger? One can never have enough anger.

PABLO: Anger doesn't belong in art.

JULIA: Of course it does. Everything belongs in art: anger, happiness, dreams, fear…

PABLO: That's not true.

JULIA: Pablo, people of African descent are treated horribly all over the world. It makes me so angry I have to write about it.

PABLO: That's good Julia, but you must transform the anger.

JULIA: I'm not sure what you mean.

PABLO: Art should come from love, not hate.

JULIA: I have to be honest with you, I don't agree. You write amazing political poems, didn't they come from anger.

PABLO: All of my poems come from love, even the political ones. Everything stems from love, love of self; love of land; love of culture; love of country, love of humanity…people who love do not oppress and support tyranny. If you want something, someone, some political system to change it's because of a love you have for a better world. Use the anger to write the poem, the anger comes from love – you should read it from love. Don't hold onto the anger. Anger will destroy your talent, it will make you bitter, it will destroy your soul. Don't ever let anger take over your heart.

JULIA: What if I'm surrounded by anger?

PABLO: Feel it, transform it and release it.

JULIA: That's not easy to do. It's almost impossible.

PABLO: You have no choice, that's what artists do. Are you working on anything now?

JULIA: Yes, I'm working on a collection, it may become two separate collections...I'm thinking of the titles CAMPOS or THE SEA AND YOU. But it's not ready at all.

PABLO: We always think it's never ready. Would you allow me to read the poems?

JULIA: Of course!! But they're rough.

PABLO: Julia...I have been very fortunate in my life for many reasons...but to witness the birth of a new artist is exciting and liberating. You're inspiring me to go home and write. I'd love to read your work.

JULIA: It'll be my pleasure. Thank you.

PABLO: If you permit me, I'd like to write an introduction to the work.

JULIA: You haven't even read the poems yet.

PABLO: I have faith in you Julia.

LIGHTS SHIFT. PABLO NERUDA exits.

WOMAN: I have faith in you too Julia.

END OF SCENE 7.

SCENE 8

PLACE: Apartment – La Havana, Cuba

> *JULIA rises from her chair and grabs a shawl and exits. The LIGHTS SHIFT INTO NIGHT. She approaches the scrim.*

JULIA: Juan….

> *She whispers loudly.*

Juan…pssst…Juan

> *JUAN appears behind the scrim in a robe.*

JUAN: Who is it?

JULIA: Julia.

JUAN: Do you know what time it is?

JULIA: I need to talk to you.

JUAN: We'll talk tomorrow.

JULIA: I need to see you now.

JUAN: Julia, go home.

JULIA: I'm not leaving until I see you…Juan…Juan come out!

> *JUAN comes out from behind the scrim with a robe on.*

JUAN: Coño Julia, you're gonna wake up the whole neighborhood.

> *JULIA hugs him and kisses him passionately. JUAN doesn't respond.*

JULIA: It feels good to touch you.

JUAN: How did you get out of the house?

JULIA: Please don't be mad Juan, I needed to see you.

JUAN: How did you get out of the house?

JULIA: I snuck out.

JUAN: You can't do that.

JULIA: I do it all the time.

JUAN: If they catch you, they'll throw you out.

JULIA: Oh that'll be such a tragedy.

She's playful.

Don't you miss me?

JUAN: I'm paying a lot of money for you to be at that place.

JULIA: I hate it there…what a stupid idea – a Boarding House for Engaged Women - the woman who runs the house is so strict with us; she treats us like children. We can't go out after a certain time – we're only allowed to sew or crochet, or listen to the radio; oh and we can talk to each other – but in low tones… we all have to eat a formal dinner at the same time every evening, and the dinner is horrible – those snotty girls insult the servants right in front of their faces…I told La Doña that, that classism is completely un-Christian-like and they should be ashamed of themselves…then we got into a big argument, and she sent me to my room. Can you believe that? To my room – I don't know who the hell she thinks she is –

JUAN: Julia you can't tell her how to run her own house.

JULIA: I can't write there - I have to write in secret in the middle of the night ….it is so fascist! I have to get out of there.

JUAN: You have no choice right now.

JULIA: But we do have choices Juan – it doesn't have to be like this.

JUAN: Listen to me – if you want to get married you have to stay in the boarding house.

JULIA: I can't stand it anymore.

JUAN: Do you want to get married?

JULIA: Of course I do.

JUAN: Then you have to stay there until we are married.

JULIA: And when is that going to be?

JUAN: I don't know yet.

JULIA: What are you waiting for?

JUAN: The right time.

JULIA: Have you told your family?

>   *Pause.*

JUAN: No.

JULIA: I've been stuck in that awful prison so that I could become respectable enough for you, and you haven't done anything about our marriage!!!

>   *Pause. JUAN doesn't answer and he turns away from her.*

JULIA: I gave up school…

>   *JUAN still doesn't look at her.*

JULIA: So why am I doing this?

JUAN: Julia you have to stay there. And you can't just stay there a couple of months…it has to be a significant amount of time.

JULIA: Why can't we just get married?

JUAN: Because I can't marry someone I was living with – they're certain rules that have to be followed, and I can't break them because you don't like them. And you knew what it was going to be like, and you agreed to it.

JULIA: But it's horrible Juan, and it's killing me; my writing is suffering. Please let me come home.

JUAN: You promised to stay there until we got married.

JULIA: Since you're NOT in a hurry to get married – I don't have to stay there OR I know what – let me come home now and when you announce the wedding I'll go back there and stay there until the wedding day.

JUAN: NO!...Julia it's late, come back tomorrow, during the day.

JULIA: How could you say you love me and do this to me?

JUAN: Look Julia, you want to be my wife this is what you have to do. This is the life I'm offering you and this is the life you will live as my wife.

JULIA: You don't want this.

JUAN: Yes I do. I don't want my wife hanging out in cafes with other men, seeing plays, drinking or reading poetry or whatever. There's only one type of woman that does that.

JULIA: Oh please come up with something original... something that required some thought.

JUAN: I want my wife to take care of me. That's what I really want. If you can't do that, you can not be with me.

JULIA: What happened to you? You've changed - we were going to be different – we were going to be the revolutionary couple and make the world a better place.

JUAN: Julia, grow up.

JULIA: The promise of revolution is that we would all do better – NOT worse. You're giving up on all our dreams.

JUAN: You want to live in a world that will never exist. You have a decision to make….are you going to do what you have to do to be my wife?

JULIA: I thought loving you was enough.

JUAN: Go back to the house. Good night.

> *JUAN motions to go back into the house. JULIA grabs his arm.*

JULIA: Don't walk away from me!

JUAN: Good night Julia!

> *He walks away.*

JULIA: How I wish I didn't love you.

END OF SCENE 8.

SCENE 9
PLACE: Cuba
TIME: 1942

> *JULIA is alone on stage.*

JULIA: AH….Why are you doing this to me? If I only I wasn't a poet…If I could just be what men wanted me to be!!…"I tried to be like men wanted me to be: an intent of life; a game of hide and seek with my being. But I was made of nows"…I was made of nows, of nows, of nows…no more…no more nows…

> *The WOMAN enters.*

WOMAN: You cannot change who you are.

JULIA: Yes I can.

WOMAN: For what? To please people who don't care about you.

JULIA: You make my life so difficult.

WOMAN: So difficult? What kind of life do you want?

JULIA: Peaceful…

WOMAN: What does peaceful mean?

JULIA: A life with no special identity, no Julia DE Burgos – just Julia Burgos – plain and simple. Take your name back – take DE Burgos back. I don't belong to you and you don't belong to me.

WOMAN: You want to belong to a man? It's about Juan?

JULIA: No.

WOMAN: I don't believe you.

JULIA: It's not only about him.

WOMAN: Oh you want to be Mrs. Grullón and serve tea to those uptight bourgeoisie fascists ladies – serve dinner promptly at six to the man of the house and have baby after baby after baby.

JULIA: Why not?! …yes I want a baby; I want to feel a baby grow inside of me BUT my body can't fulfill my desire. I feel so empty. I want to create something in this world.

WOMAN: You write poetry.

JULIA: It's not coming anymore, and what comes out is terrible. I sit down to write and I'm empty. There's nothing.

WOMAN: You're not letting the poetry in.

JULIA: It's not right…something's wrong.

WOMAN: You're depressed Julia.

JULIA: I'm scared.

WOMAN: You're not letting yourself hear OR see OR feel.

JULIA: I feel too much and it hurts. Stop the pain.

WOMAN: I don't know how.

JULIA: I have no one.

WOMAN: I'm here!

JULIA: I want to go home.

WOMAN: We can't go home.

JULIA: I miss my family. I'm so lonely.

WOMAN: You have lots of friends.

JULIA: You have faith in people and then they disappoint you. I can't find Pablo Neruda; he probably didn't mean it, about writing the introduction for me. Why should he waste his time?!...Let's go to Puerto Rico now.

WOMAN: Julia we can't.

JULIA: I want to walk on my land, swim in my river, touch my family.

WOMAN: It's not safe for you. The government is becoming more hostile towards patriots.

JULIA: It's safe for ME. I just want to live a simple life. But you want to start trouble and change all the rules. You have to go. I'm tired of you controlling me! I'm in control here – you're only my soul. I am ripping you out of me and putting you in this music box and throwing you in the river.

JULIA takes MUSIC BOX and removes a poem from it.

WOMAN: Don't do it.

The WOMAN tries to grab the music box from JULIA.

JULIA: Give it to me.

WOMAN: It's a mistake to do this. You can't have peace if you tear us apart!

JULIA: "The madness of my soul cannot be still,
      it lives in anxiety, in the disorder,
      in the imbalance of things dynamic,
      in the silence of the free thinker,
      who lives alone, in quiet exile..."
I'm going to bury you in this music box!

WOMAN: Please, don't do it!

JULIA: ...My soul? How I want to control her, adapt her, remake her…

JULIA kisses the poem and puts it in the music box.

WOMAN: No, Julia, I'm begging you!

JULIA: And...destroy her!

WOMAN: AH!

      BLACKOUT.

END OF SCENE 9.

END OF ACT I.

46

ACT II

SCENE 1
PLACE: A COFFEE HOUSE - NEW YORK CITY –
TIME: 1949

> *THE TABLE AND THE SOFA DOUBLE FOR*
> *FURNITURE THAT WOULD TYPICALLY BE*
> *FOUND IN A POETRY CAFÉ.*

> *The stage is dark. A spot light shines down-stage*
> *center. Applause is heard. The WOMAN appears*
> *out of the darkness.*

ANNOUNCER/VOICE-OVER: Our next poet is Julia de
Burgos.

> *Applause.*

WOMAN: "People are saying that I am your enemy
        because in verse I give the world your I.
        They lie, Julia de Burgos.
        They lie, Julia de Burgos.
        The one who speaks in my verse
        is not your voice.
        It is my voice…
        Because you are the dressing
        and the essence am I;
        and the most profound abyss
        stretches between the two.
        You are the cold doll of social lies,
        and I, the virile sparkle of human truth.
        You, honey of courtesan hypocrisies;
        not I; who in all my poems bare my heart.
        You are like your world, egotistical;
        not I; I gamble everything to be who I am.

> *There is a small light on the WOMAN. As the poem*
> *progresses the light becomes brighter around her.*

You are the grave, ladylike lady; not I;
I am life, strength, woman.
You belong to your husband, to your master; not I;
I belong to nobody, or to everyone,
because to everyone, to everyone
I give myself in my pure feeling and thought.

You curl your hair and paint your face; not me;
the wind curls my hair, the sun paints my face.
You are a housewife, resigned, submissive,
tied to the prejudices of men; not I;
I am Rocinante racing wildly seeking
the horizons of God's justice.

You do not govern yourself;
everyone governs you; your husband, your parents,
your relatives, the priest, the dressmaker,
the theatre, the casino, the car,
your jewels, the banquet, champagne, heaven
and hell, and society's, 'what will they say.'
Not in me, only my heart rules me,
only my thoughts; who rules in me is I.

You, flower of aristocracy;
and I, a flower of the people.

You have everything and to everyone owe it,
while I, my nothing to no one do I owe.
You, nailed to your static ancestral dividend,
and I, just a number in the cipher
of the social divisor,
are the duel to that death that fatally approaches."

*JULIA enters – she has on the tattered coat from the
first act. She is tired and her voice is hoarse.*

JULIA: Stop it!

WOMAN: "When the masses run riotous
　　　　leaving behind ashes of burned injustices,
　　　　and when, with the torches of the seven virtues…"

JULIA: What are you doing?

The WOMAN moves away from Julia – Julia pursues her and tries to pull her away.

WOMAN: "…the masses pursue the seven sins,"

JULIA: Stop reading!!

WOMAN: "…against you, and against all the unjust and inhuman,"

JULIA: What the hell are you doing?

WOMAN: "…I will be in their midst with the torch in my hand."

APPLAUSE is heard.

WOMAN: Thank you…thank you…

JULIA: Stop it!! All of you STOP IT!!

WOMAN: They love you Julia…listen to them.

JULIA: STOP IT!!

WOMAN: NO!

JULIA: Why are you doing this to me?

WOMAN: I was just reading poetry.

JULIA: You are never to read my poetry again.

JULIA takes the poem out of the WOMAN's hand and rips it up. The WOMAN picks up the pieces of the poem.

WOMAN: You throw me away and you try to destroy us – I have a right!!

JULIA: You have no right! I don't want you back. You are never to read my poetry!!

WOMAN: You have no choice, you heard the words and YOU came back to ME!

JULIA: I came back to stop you; I want to forget the words – I want to forget you.

WOMAN: Let me back in Julia.

JULIA: No! I don't want to live your life.

WOMAN: You had your chance Julia, you threw me out – and you lived – how did you live, were you happy, peaceful? Juan threw you out – bought you the ticket and sent you on a boat to Miami. That's not living…you were broken.

JULIA: I don't trust you. I let you back in my life in Washington D.C. and it was a disaster.

WOMAN: That wasn't my fault.

JULIA: Yes it was. You can't be trusted.

END OF SCENE 1.

SCENE 2:
PLACE: Apartment – Washington D.C.
TIME: Late 40s.

> *Lights Shift. JULIA is cleaning the table and
> straightening up the room. The WOMAN enters.*

WOMAN: Well hello Mrs. Marín.

JULIA: You're late.

WOMAN: I had other appointments…Can I come in?

JULIA: Come in.

WOMAN: Nice house.

JULIA: Thank you.

WOMAN: I was surprised that you contacted me.

JULIA: I wanted to see you.

WOMAN: And thank you for seeing me Mrs. Marín.

JULIA: Stop calling me that.

WOMAN: Isn't that your new name?

JULIA: Yes…stop it.

WOMAN: Aren't you happy being somebody's wife?

JULIA: Look, I wanted to see you – you don't have to be sarcastic.

WOMAN: Ooh, sensitive – I thought you were giving up sensitivity.

JULIA: Would you stop it! I really want to talk to you.

WOMAN: Okay, okay, sorry…but you have to understand something – I've been abandoned, lost, frustrated…

JULIA: If you would just behave.

WOMAN: You know – have a nice life!

The WOMAN gets up to leave.

JULIA: Don't go…please.

WOMAN: What do you want?

JULIA: Just sit down, let's talk…here, have some tea.

\WOMAN: Tea…oh...how nice…okay.

JULIA pours tea and they sit on the sofa. Pause.

WOMAN: Do you like Washington D.C?

JULIA: It's…it's okay, it's better than okay. Armando and I are happy here.

WOMAN: White picket fence – congratulations – you got what you wanted - convention.

JULIA: Yes, I did…and it feels great.

WOMAN: Why did you invite me here?

JULIA: I wanted you to see that I'm okay.

WOMAN: Good for you…Where's Mr. Marín?

JULIA: He's working.

WOMAN: What does he do?

JULIA: He's an accountant.

WOMAN: Oh…so safe.

JULIA: Yes, I have a safe life; I worked hard to get it.

WOMAN: Congratulations…again…safe…so you got yourself a safe man. Do you love him?

JULIA: …Yes…

WOMAN: Hm…you don't love him.

JULIA: I do.

WOMAN: You can't lie to me.

JULIA: He's a good man.

WOMAN: Has Juan contacted you?

JULIA: Why are you asking me that?

WOMAN: Small talk over tea – isn't that what married ladies do?

JULIA: Talking about ex-loves is inappropriate.

WOMAN: I don't know the difference between appropriate and inappropriate, forgive me. Can I have some more tea?

JULIA pours more tea. Pause.

JULIA: He wrote me a letter.

WOMAN: What did he want?

JULIA: I don't know I didn't read it. I threw it out.

WOMAN: You didn't read it.

JULIA: No.

WOMAN: …You still love Juan.

JULIA: No I don't. I don't want to have anything to do with him.

WOMAN: If you can't even read his letter, he still has your heart.

JULIA: I'm married now – that was all in the past.

WOMAN: If he walked in through that door right now, what would you do?

JULIA: I don't want to talk about it…

WOMAN: Julia, you're living without love.

JULIA: I said I don't want to talk about it.

Pause.

WOMAN: Well?

JULIA: Well what?

WOMAN: I'm here, I see you're doing great, you're happy and safe…what do you want me to do?

JULIA: I was thinking…maybe we could start writing together again.

The WOMAN is stunned – she begins laughing.

WOMAN: Do you think you're doing me a favor?

JULIA: That's not why I'm asking.

WOMAN: You got everything you want, so it's okay for me to come back?

JULIA: You're making it sound like that's something bad.

WOMAN: Do you mean it?

JULIA: Yes.

WOMAN: Are you sure?

JULIA: Yes, I feel strong enough for you.

WOMAN: Are you absolutely sure?

JULIA: Yes.

WOMAN: Good…I was praying that you were going to ask me back.

JULIA: I'm glad you think so.

WOMAN: There's a lot of work that needs to be done. I can't believe you live right in the heart of Washington D.C.

JULIA: Not right in the heart.

WOMAN: It doesn't matter, we could do so much.

JULIA: What?

WOMAN: Do you know that Albizu Campos was arrested again? So was Juan Antonio Corretjer…after the Nationalist shooting at Blair House; everyone in D.C. is on edge. You are so brilliant. A house in Washington D.C. – Right under their noses. No one would ever think to look here.

JULIA: Wait, wait, what are you talking about?

WOMAN: We definitely have to start writing again BUT Julia this place is perfect.

JULIA: For what?

WOMAN: For meetings of course.

JULIA: What meetings?

WOMAN: For the Partido...we have to raise money for the political prisoners.

JULIA: No. I'm not involved with politics anymore.

WOMAN: Julia this is important! What are you doing all day? Cleaning, Cooking.

JULIA: Yes, I am keeping my home, but I'm also studying typing – I'm going to apply for a job as a secretary.

WOMAN: Look Julia, I know you've been away for a while – but we could do a lot...

JULIA: I said NO! This is not why I brought you back.

WOMAN: Julia you have the perfect set up.

JULIA: Armando won't like it.

WOMAN: I'm not Mrs. Marín.

JULIA: NO! It's dangerous, I'm not doing it!

WOMAN: Look I'll take care of everything – you just take care of Armando – Trust me.

JULIA: I don't have a good feeling about this.

WOMAN: Don't be scared.

JULIA: Slow down, why do you have to go to the extreme immediately?

WOMAN: I'm not.

JULIA: You couldn't wait five minutes to start with your….

WOMAN: Julia, it's going to be okay – I'll make it right.

JULIA: You're right about one thing. Washington D.C. is completely on alert. This Senator McCarthy is starting all this trouble. He's going after anyone that's a "communist" – even if they are progressive – he considers them communists. And for this government, being a Nationalist is worse than being a Communist…YOU want to go and do something foolish.

WOMAN: We're just going to raise money.

JULIA: I'm not taking a chance like that…this was supposed to be an opportunity for us to get closer. That's all I want, I don't want any trouble.

WOMAN: …I know that.

JULIA: We're going to go one step at a time….okay.

WOMAN: Yes I know, BUT together we'll be strong.

JULIA: Promise you won't do anything rash…Promise…

WOMAN: …okay…

JULIA: Promise ME.

WOMAN: Yes, okay I promise.

   Lights Shift

END OF SCENE 2.

SCENE 3

PLACE: Coffee Houses / Poetry Cafes throughout the D.C. area.

Woman/Soul enters. There is a tight spotlight on her.

WOMAN: This poem is entitled AWAKEN, and I dedicate it to the Puerto Rican woman in her hour of transcendence....

> "...Woman,
> you, who often purges
> the bitter melodies of your soul...
> you who feels,
> you who suffers,
> you who cries in bitter solitude...
> Don't you feel the anguish?
> Don't you hear the cries
> of your children,
> of your soul,
> of your homeland
> demanding freedom?..."

Lights Shift.

WOMAN: For a great man, whom I am admire so much...who finds himself, once again in federal prison, for fighting for the freedom of our beloved island, Puerto Rico - A SONG FOR ALBIZU CAMPOS...

> "...Prince of the empire of constellations
> where the soul begins to create an idea...
> Heart of the moment, nerve and pulse of the world
> that lived in your martyrdom,
> through you, are set FREE.
> In your prison, the defeated people saw themselves and
> in your name, the people, now redeemed, arrive..."

Lights Shift.

WOMAN: Good evening, My name is Julia de Burgos...For my fellow brothers and sisters who are on strike....WE ARE CLOSED FISTS...

"...We strike on the docks.
Unloading the centuries of your man-machine;
we are no longer slaves.
Unloading the history of the voice of the rich;
we now speak.
Unloading the system of the laws that exploit;
we now think.
Continue the strike comrades:
We are no longer slaves!
We announce the cry of the NOW:
We are closed fists!"

Julia raises her fist. Blackout.

END OF SCENE 3.

SCENE 4
PLACE: Apartment

As lights rise...JULIA is picking up a mess in the living room. The WOMAN enters.

WOMAN: I just heard about the raid.

JULIA: The F.B.I. destroyed everything. Armando was brought in for questioning.

WOMAN: Are you okay?

JULIA: You promised me you wouldn't do something foolish.

WOMAN: It was just a couple of meetings.

JULIA: Meetings? You read about a poem about ALBIZU CAMPOS! What's the matter with you?! Didn't you understand me, when I told you about how the Nationalists are being treated?

WOMAN: I didn't want to upset you.

JULIA: You lied to me.

WOMAN: I didn't mean for this to happen.

JULIA: Someone could have gotten hurt.

WOMAN: But no one did.

JULIA: The point is that you lied to me. I knew it...I knew something like this would happen. Once again I'm cleaning up a mess you created. You can't be trusted.

WOMAN: Julia I swear, I didn't want this to happen.

JULIA: You don't care about anyone else, but yourself. Armando thinks we should move to his mother's house in New Jersey. I agree with him. I was a fool to think we could make it work. I don't want to be a revolutionary. I don't want to change the world. Mami was right. Things cannot be changed.

WOMAN: I'm sorry. I didn't want to ruin your life.

JULIA: Grow up already.

> *The WOMAN exits while JULIA is still picking up the mess. After a few beats JULIA notices the emptiness and looks up and realizes that she's gone.*

JULIA: Good...just go.

> *JULIA goes over to the music box and hums the song. LIGHTS SHIFT TO PRESENT 1953.*

END OF SCENE 4.

SCENE 5
PLACE: Apartment – New York - 1953

JULIA: If only you hadn't pushed so hard.

WOMAN: If only you weren't afraid – I could have given you strength.

JULIA: I thought that was it. I thought I'd never see you again.

WOMAN: I was broken without you Julia and it hurt so much. I wanted you to suffer the way I did. All these years I felt your pain…and I was happy. I wanted you to feel the pain I felt. I wanted you to pay for your fear.

Lights Shift. What follows will be a theatrical montage.

VOICE-OVER: "…What are they waiting for?
        Why don't they call me?
        have you forgotten me among the grasses,
        my humble comrades, the dead of the Earth?
        Why don't the bells ring?
        I'm ready to go.
        perhaps they want more cadavers
        of dreams, dead of innocence?…"

PART I: PUBLISHING OFFICE

JULIA enters the apartment in a hurry. She takes off her coat and moves the round table down-stage center. JULIA enters a publishing office. There is a man behind the scrim. LIGHTS SHOULD BE STARK AND SCARY.

JULIA: This is a new collection. It has some old poems that I wrote in Puerto Rico and Cuba…but basically they've never been published.

PUBLISHER: Julia, I'm not looking for new work to publish.

JULIA: Like I said, they're some old poems in this collection – it's called THE SEA AND YOU. What do you think?

PUBLISHER: Julia listen, I'm not interested.

JULIA: But you always loved my work.

PUBLISHER: I know, but now is not a good time.

JULIA: What do you mean good time?

PUBLISHER: We can't take a risk publishing anyone connected to any political organizations.

JULIA: I'm not – I'm not doing any political work anymore.

PUBLISHER: But you did once.

JULIA: That was a while ago.

PUBLISHER: It doesn't matter – it's not good business.

JULIA: I really need this publication…

PUBLISHER: I'm sorry Julia.

JULIA: Just read the poems. They're only love poems. Not one about war and Albizu Campos or anything like that.

PUBLISHER: Aren't you writing for the newspaper, PUEBLOS HISPANOS?

JULIA: …Sometimes…

PUBLISHER: Isn't the editor a Nationalist?

JULIA: Juan Antonio Corretjer, he's out of jail, the government doesn't see him as a threat anymore…so there's no problem.

PUBLISHER: You still don't understand; it doesn't matter. The answer is NO. I can't afford to lose my business. Maybe in a couple of years – when the political climate is less hostile.

JULIA: I have no money.

PUBLISHER: I'm sorry Julia. There's nothing I can do.

Lights Shift.

VOICE-OVER: "…Perhaps they want more rubbish
        from wilted springtimes
        more dry eyes in the clouds
        more faces, wounded in the storms?
        Do they want the wind's coffin
        crouching in my tangled hair?
        Do they want the brook's yearning,
        to die in my poet's mind?…"

Lights Shift.

PART II: FACTORY

> *JULIA gets a bag of fabric and puts it on the table. She tries to organize the pieces and starts to hand sew one of them. A figure appears from behind the scrim. This is the factory foreman. [She can be played by the woman who played Julia's mother.] She remains behind the scrim. JULIA'S VOICE IS VERY HOARSE AND SHE FREQUENTLY COUGHS THROUGHOUT THESE SCENES.*

BOSS: Hey Burgos, you're late again.

JULIA: I'm sorry; I've been sick…I had pneumonia…

BOSS: I don't run a hospital here.

JULIA: I'm sorry; I won't do it again.

BOSS: That's what you've said every damn day you've worked here. You're costing me money. You're fired.

JULIA: I couldn't leave the hospital.

BOSS: That's not my problem.

JULIA: I need this job.

BOSS: So do dozens of other people.

JULIA: I'll work double shifts.

BOSS: I said you're fired! Get out.

> *JULIA doesn't move.*

JULIA: What am I going to do?

BOSS: That's your problem…I need the space for somebody else…Get going.

JULIA slowly puts her coat on and begins to walk away – she then grabs an armful of fabric and throws it on the scrim. The fabric should remain on the floor.

PUBLISHER: There's nothing I can do.

JULIA: AHHHH!! I don't care about your stupid job; I'll get another one – I always get another job.

JULIA runs off-stage left. The lights behind the scrim goes black. JULIA re-enters on stage-right.

VOICE-OVER: "...Do they want the sun dismantled, and consumed in my arteries?..."

Lights Shift.

PART III: OUTSIDE OF A BUILDING

A super appears from behind the scrim. THE LIGHTING IS STARK AND HARSH. They are fighting.

JULIA: Would you give me a chance to explain?

SUPER: I don't want any explanations.

JULIA: You have no right to do this.

SUPER: Listen lady, you owe me six months rent. You got it on you?

JULIA: No...not right now. But I'm getting a new job with a newspaper; I'm writing articles...

SUPER: You a writer?

JULIA: Yes.

SUPER: How about writing me a check?

JULIA: As soon as I get some...

SUPER: Goodbye.

JULIA: I'm working on getting some new work. It's just I had an operation on my throat and…

SUPER: I don't care! Get out!

BOSS: Get going!

PUBLISHER: There's nothing I can do!

TOGETHER: Get out!

> *THE SUPER exits stage-left. She starts throwing books and clothes into the main playing area center stage. JULIA runs onto stage.*

VOICE-OVER: "... Do they want the shadow of my shadow,
    where not one star remains?
    I can barely endure this world
    that beats my entire conscience…"

> *Lights Shift.*

PART IV: POETRY CAFÉ

> *JULIA enters the apartment, which is a poetry café again. She's in another overcoat and looks dirty. She's coughing a lot and is a little drunk. There is a man already seated at the table – which is still on down stage center.*

JULIA: Look who's here…Tito Arroyo…ARRRRRoyo….
A-RRO-YO….Tito -- where have you been?

TITO: Julia…um…are you okay? Sit down…

JULIA: Pues m'ijo… Coño, I haven't seen you in a long time…

TITO: You haven't been to the last poetry readings…you know we've missed you…

JULIA: As you can see, I've been busy -- you know, doing this and that AND other things…You have any new poems? I'd love to hear them…You know you can always read them to me if you want some criticism….

TITO: I know…Julia, it's after midnight, let me take you home.

JULIA: YOU don't you want to talk to me!

TITO: Julia it's late….

JULIA: I just want to talk to you, that's all…I just want to talk, I want to talk like we used to, you know …Tito …I've missed you.

TITO: Tomorrow Julia; we'll talk tomorrow.

JULIA: No, I want to talk now, …come on,

> *JULIA takes a seat.*

JULIA: So, um, read your most recent poem to me…Hey do you want a drink? Hello waiter?! Hey, we want a drink…

TITO: Julia keep it down.

JULIA: Okay, okay…here…look I'll write you a poem.
She writes something on a napkin really fast.
Like old times.

> *She gives it to Tito.*

I haven't written for a while but…Okay, well, good to see you. See you at the next meeting of writers. I promise I'll be there.

> *She goes to exit.*

Oh…you can give me five dollars.

TITO: What?

JULIA: Okay – fifty cents.

TITO: If you need money I can give…

JULIA: No, no, I just want you to pay me for the poem.

TITO: Okay.

> *TITO gives her money.*

JULIA: This is too much…BUT okay I'll take it. I'll write you another one tomorrow. Bye, bye. Thanks so much.

JULIA exits. She knocks down a chair. JULIA doesn't pick it up. TITO reads poem.

TITO: "Goodbye…The miserable star of the earth tells us goodbye …The misery star that delights in her misery…"
Ave Maria Julia…I can't run after you anymore.

TITO looks at poem.

Okay…

TITO gets up and exits quickly.

Julia…Julia...

Lights Shift.

VOICE-OVER: "…Give me my number! I don't want
        love to leave me…
        constant dreams that follow me
        as footprints follow my steps…."

JULIA re-enters collapses in a mess of clothes and books.

JULIA: Oh…and my soul says I don't fight! How the hell am I supposed to fight like this?!

She looks around and picks up some books.

Why doesn't she fight for me? Why doesn't she come here and deal with this mess – she causes the mess but OH NO, she won't deal with the consequences…and now I'm stuck in this awful basement…I need this one – *The Magic Mountain*, Thomas Mann wrote this book for me…I want to go into the asylum and disappear inside the magic mountain, where nobody will ever find me.

VOICE-OVER: "…Give me my number, because if not,
        I will die after death!"

Pause. JULIA lays down on the books.

JULIA: "Give me my number, or else I will die after death!"

Lights fade.

END OF SCENE 5.

SCENE 6
PLACE: The Apartment -- 1953

> *The mess of clothing, books and a knocked down chair remain. JULIA is sleeping on top of all of this mess. As lights rise she starts to stir. The light should be the sun filtering in through the window. The light will begin behind the scrim. JULIA gets up with difficulty. She is limping a bit and has a pain in her stomach. She sits on the sofa and hugs her stomach. Her health has deteriorated. She then gets up and walks with difficulty to the table and pours herself a drink. Walks extreme downstage and looks out into the audience as if looking through a window.*

> *The WOMAN is behind the scrim.*

JULIA: Ah Consuelo, dear sister, I so want to go back to Puerto Rico. I want to go back to Río Grande de Loiza and dive right in…I just want to dive in and feel the water caress my body – be a fish and swim all the way to the ocean. My dear sister "this rootlessness/exile I find myself in, wandering from country to country from defeat/failure to defeat…It is a pain situated in death…" My soul has found me Consuelo…she doesn't leave me alone…she's haunting me again. I thought all dreams would be over after she was gone – but she's back and the dreams are coming back. My dreams have become nightmares. She said I wasn't writing and that I gave up. She's right. But I can do it again.…Hm…I was the writer, not her…who does she think she is? Her enemy?! – she thinks I'm her enemy. Just watch miss Julia de Burgos…It is my voice that gave life to you…

> *PLEASE NOTE THAT JULIA IS SICK – NOT DRUNK. She frantically looks for paper and a pencil.*

JULIA: Where is the pencil? I was just writing the other day.

Julia crawls on the floor looking for a pencil/pen. She looks under the sofa, then she looks in between the cushions. She finds an old pencil. As she walks back to the table she is sharpening the pencil first with her fingernails, then with her teeth.

JULIA: Okay,…I'm gonna write the best poem ever written – better than Río Grande de Loíza –
She tries to write something.

"The Moon…" Okay, forget the moon.
She writes something else.

JULIA: "The sun…shining in despair" …no, no, no, no …no sun or moon – that's stupid…

JULIA crumples the paper and throws it on the floor. She realizes that she doesn't have another piece of paper. She goes to the bureau and finds no paper. Then JULIA picks up the crumbled paper and starts to unfold it.

JULIA: No, I can't do this…

The WOMAN enters.

WOMAN: Keep going.

JULIA: I can't.

WOMAN: Don't stop!

JULIA: Stop pushing me!! It's not there anymore.

WOMAN: Yes it is.

JULIA: Stop it, God, you keep on pushing and pushing. I can't do this.

WOMAN: Yes you can.

JULIA: No, I can't.

WOMAN: Let yourself fly Julia.

JULIA: It's a curse – this longing to write – I don't want it. I don't want my life doomed to that curse.

WOMAN: It was your destiny.

JULIA: You have too much passion – you burned me out.

WOMAN: I'm sorry I didn't know how to care without being passionate...strong...challenging. It was a sweet curse.

JULIA: I would have given up that 'sweet curse" for a family any day. It's too painful.

WOMAN: You're right, the pain is great because the joys are greater.

JULIA: There's not much joy.

WOMAN: Don't tell me it didn't feel good to have Pablo Neruda tell you that you were called to be the great poet of Latin America?! Come on – It felt good!
   Pause.
How about reading poetry – and those eyes fixated on you and for a brief moment, you have taken the audience on a journey – to Río Grande de Loiza; to a field of flowers; to the streets of the Ponce Massacre, the massacres in Russia and China; and the Spanish Civil War...You hold them in the palm of your hands – you are their guide.

JULIA: ...I want to stop all my feelings.

WOMAN: Then you have to being so sensitive! Stop feeling for people – stop feeling the sorrow of oppression around the world; stop feeling the sadness of humanity; the triumph of joy... Stop feeling!! You can't...no matter how hard you tried you couldn't stop your feelings. That's what I use to write poetry... I cannot make poetry without your feelings; your senses. I need you to write. I was broken too Julia! I need your pain, your suffering, your anger, your love, your joy. Without your highs - without your lows – without your politics and

69

compassion I could not write – I can't write without you – I'm a poet without words – I am dead without you.

JULIA: NO! Leave me. I have nothing left to give to you.

> *JULIA gets the music box.*

JULIA: You are not me! We are not one! We want different things; we travel different paths…YOU should have never found me!! You belong in this box!

> *JULIA opens the box – she hums the song from the music box.*

JULIA: Come on sing the song…come on – did you forget it? - Let me remind you.

> *JULIA hums the song.*

WOMAN: Shut up.

> *JULIA sings louder.*

WOMAN: Shut up!

> *JULIA sings even louder.*

WOMAN: I said shut up!

JULIA: Come on JULIA! Sing…

> *JUAN GRULLÓN enters and startles JULIA. The WOMAN retreats upstage but remains in the scene. Lights shift.*

JUAN: Julia.

JULIA: Juan…

END OF SCENE 6.

SCENE 7
PLACE: HOSPITAL - 1953

> *JULIA slowly walks over picks up a book and goes to the rocking chair, sits in it and begins to rock. She coughs slightly and she again has great difficulty breathing BUT it is the worst it has ever been. The rocking chair is downstage and faces the audience. Julia sits in it and begins to rock. The LIGHTS ARE BRIGHT –REFLECTING DAY LIGHT. The singing of birds is heard.*

JUAN: Hello. Julia, can I speak to you?

JULIA: Juan…

JUAN: Julia, I'm going to be in New York for only one week. I'd like to speak to you.

> *JUAN pulls up a chair next to her. He tries to kiss her on the cheek. She doesn't respond.*

JULIA: Don't.

JUAN: It's good to see you.

> *JULIA coughs.*

JUAN: Are you okay?

> *JULIA'S voice is hoarse.*

JULIA: I had some polyps in my throat removed.

JUAN: Are you better?

JULIA: A little.

JUAN: Do you need anything?

> *He starts to fuss with her blanket.*

JULIA: No. What are you doing here?

JUAN: I'm giving a conference. I didn't know if you were still living in New York...Where is your husband?

JULIA: I don't know; we're separated. Where's your wife?

JUAN: How did you know?

JULIA: I hear she's rich and older – and Spaniard. Be careful with those Spaniards though – you know the Moors were in Spain for eight hundred years and sometimes a little grifa pops up when you least expect it.

JUAN: That was one of the reasons why I fell in love with you – your fighting spirit.

> *Pause.*

You look beautiful.

JULIA: I look horrible.

JUAN: To be honest I thought you would look worse.

JULIA: What do you want Juan?

JUAN: ...I've been thinking about you...I can't get you out of my mind...how about I take you out of here?

JULIA: And what?

JUAN: I'll take care of you.

JULIA: I don't think you know what you're saying.

JUAN: I do...we can make a life for ourselves.

JULIA: Where?

JUAN: We could live in New York.

JULIA: I'd rather live in Puerto Rico.

JUAN: Puerto Rico sounds great.

JULIA: Oh really?!

JUAN: I made a mistake Julia, I was wrong…

>*JULIA doesn't respond.*

JUAN: I am so sorry for what I did to you.

JULIA: You think by saying 'sorry' and promising me some make-believe life together – I'm supposed to jump and hug and kiss you?!! You actually believe that you can make my life better. What about your wife? I'm too old to be a secret.

JUAN: You wouldn't be. I don't love her; I love you.

JULIA: Just you and me?

JUAN: Yes…I'll divorce her; I promise.

>*Pause.*

JULIA: *(quietly)* No.

JUAN: No? Julia I'm offering you a life.

JULIA: I have my own. I might not have lived it the way everybody else wanted me to, but it was my life…almost my life.

JUAN: I want to take you out of here.

JULIA: I'm ill – you can't take care of me.

JUAN: Julia...I never stopped loving you.

JULIA: …In another time and place I would have loved to have heard those words, but not now, they mean nothing to me…

JUAN: I don't believe you.

JULIA: It's too late.

JUAN: No, Julia, it's not…It's not too late for us to be together.

JULIA: I want you to leave.

JUAN: Julia…we could still have a life together.

JULIA: I said leave.

> *JULIA throws her book at JUAN*

JUAN: I'll come back when you're not so angry.

JULIA: Don't!

JUAN: Julia I really…

JULIA: Don't come back ever again.

> *JUAN goes to kiss her forehead, JULIA pushes him away.*

JULIA: GO!

> *JUAN exits. JULIA starts crying.*

END OF SCENE 7.

SCENE 8
PLACE: HOSPITAL IN NEW YORK
TIME: 1953

JULIA: Ah the sun…"The sun is shining in despair at my sorrowful heart…"

> *The WOMAN approaches JULIA as she rocks in her chair.*

WOMAN: Your heart is not sorrowful; it is free.

JULIA: I wasted my life.

WOMAN: No, you lived a full life despite all the fear. You wrote great poetry – saw some of the world…And you loved with all of your heart. How many people can say they've really loved? Even as Mrs. Marín you gave 100 percent...I'm so proud of you.

JULIA: Why?

WOMAN: You fought back and the poetry returned. You never stopped feeling - you never stopped loving...hating...caring – that's why I never died...

JULIA: Yes.

JULIA softly laughs to herself.

JULIA: "When everything awakens the lilies will announce it...they will say: "It is the fatal conscience of that girl, she had many sins because she always lived in verse..."

WOMAN: I hope they all say that!!... "You will always be a poem, Julia de Burgos, the one that has nothing of a bourgeois, the one that breaks centuries in her clothes, and frees her life throughout the stars!" That was all you!!

JULIA: Us.

WOMAN: Us.

JULIA: I never wanted us to...

WOMAN: Sh! I know.

JULIA: I just wanted peace.

WOMAN: I know.

JULIA: Why come and find me at all?

WOMAN: I can't go ON without you. I need you.

JULIA: "It has to be from here, right this instance, my cry into the world...It has to be from here, forgotten but unshaken, among comrades of silence deep into Welfare Island my farewell to the world."

WOMAN: "One day I will go to dance with you to a faraway place where no law exists, nor reason rules; where the water is breeze, where the bird is flower; where everything pure and natural is fused with God's grace…"

> *THEY TAKE ONE LAST LOOK AT THE STAGE. A*
> *BODY WITH AN OVERCOAT IS ON THE FLOOR.*
> *THE LIGHTS SLOWLY FADE ON THIS BODY –*
> *JULIA DE BURGOS' LAST EARTHLY MOMENT.*

END OF SCENE 8.

SCENE 9
PLACE: RIO GRANDE DE LOÍZA

> *JULIA TAKES WOMAN'S. HAND – THE LIGHTS*
> *SHIFT INTO A BRIGHT SUN LIGHT – A FOREST*
> *APPEARS BEHIND THE SCRIM – THIS IS THE*
> *SAME IMAGE THAT WAS SEEN AT THE*
> *BEGINNING OF THE PLAY.*

> *JULIA starts to walk healthy and gracefully. Her*
> *speech becomes very fluid. She is no longer coughing*
> *and breathing heavily.*

JULIA: Where are we?

WOMAN: In Puerto Rico.

JULIA: What a beautiful river, I recognize it.

WOMAN: Of course, it's your Río Grande de Loíza, "Río Grande de Loíza…Blue. Brown. Red. Blue Mirror, fallen piece of sky…Great river…Great sorrow…The greatest of all the island's sorrow…"

JULIA: Who are these people?

> *JULIA looking out into the audience.*

WOMAN: They came to the river for you.

JULIA: For me…

WOMAN: Yes.

JULIA: What are they doing?

WOMAN: It's a tribute.

JULIA: A tribute?

WOMAN: It's a tribute for your life… Julia, it's time to go.

JULIA: *(To Audience.)* "Don't remember me!"

WOMAN: *(To Audience.)* "Feel me!"

> *They hold hands and walk together toward the river as the poem is being read. They pick up lilies and throw them into the river – which is in the downstage area. After the lilies are thrown in – THEY EXIT BEHIND THE SCRIM.*

WOMAN: "I will discard paths that are burrowed within me like roots…I am going to lose stars/ and dew/ and small streams…Tell me, what is left of the world, what?…How will I be called when all I have left is to remember myself on the rock of a deserted island?…

JULIA: "…they will call me Poet."

> *Light fade to Black.*

END OF SCENE 9.

END OF PLAY

GLOSSARY OF POEMS

A special thank you to Lcda María Consuelo Saez Burgos for her unconditional faith in trusting CHILD OF WATER with Julia's words.

ACKNOWLEDGMENTS

In 1998, I was commissioned by the Puerto Rican Traveling Theatre to write a play about Julia de Burgos. Upon hearing the news I was overwhelmed with joy, then quickly terror set it. Julia de Burgos is an icon, Puerto Rican and Feminist SHero and literary genius. How would I be able to dramatize her life? At the beginning of the writing process I was paralyzed for several months.

As I studied her poetry, interviewed people who knew her and scholars who researched her work, I slowly discovered a human being underneath all the layers of her mythology. Julia, the Woman emerged -- not only a Woman who was angry at the cruelties of the world; a Woman who believed that Social Justice and Freedom were basic human rights; a Woman who demanded that Women have an equal voice in society; a Woman who believed that the world could be a more loving and just place...but, also a Woman who loved too deeply; a Woman who longed to be a mother; a Woman who was fascinated by words and ideas; a Woman who fought tooth and nail for what she believed. She was a Woman who loved laughing and didn't stop herself from crying; a Woman far too sensitive for this harsh world -- who saw, felt and heard all too clearly. Julia's sensitivities plagued her and caused her to doubt her gift. As witnessed through her work, she could never reconcile the Woman with the Artist. I posit that these two sides of her psyche were frequently at odds throughout her lifetime. Once this level of consciousness opened up for me, JULIA DE BURGOS: CHILD OF WATER began to take shape.

In 1999, the play opened Off-Broadway and was a critical and commercial success. It is included in the archives at the Lincoln Center Library for the Performing Arts. The blessings that this play has brought to my life, still live with me as I write this - Julia's raw and intellectual power in her poetry inspire me as a writer to always take chances and look beyond boundaries and her courage to live life on her own terms, inspire me to challenge the limited conventions society has created for Women.

I would like to thank the following individuals and institutions for their assistance in writing JULIA DE BURGOS: CHILD OF WATER: Cándido Tirado, Susana Cabañas, Lcda. María Consuelo Saez Burgos, José Federico Burgos, Jr., Centro de Estudios Puertorriqueño, Hunter College, La Casa de la Herencia Cultural Puertorriqueña, Otilio Diaz, Dr. Edgar Martínez Masdeu, Roberto Ramos Perea, El Ateneo Puertorriqueño, Carmen D'Lucca, Anita Vélez Mitchell, Erica Hestel, Margarita Morales (PRTT), Municipio de Carolina, Ovidio Ajusto Rosario, Biblioteca Electrónica de Carolina, Wanda Rivera, Andrés Rivera, Mausoleo de Julia de Burgos, Oscar Morales, Juana Carrero, my aunt and guide en Carolina.

I would like to give a special thanks to Iris Morales and Red Sugarcane Press for publishing this play and bringing the life and work of a great artist to a new audience. Iris, your world-view, curiosity, intellect, friendship and spirit have enriched my life beyond words. ¡Bendición!

Julia de Burgos was a Poet; an Activist; a Revolutionary; a Woman and a Citizen of the World. ¡Qué viva Julia!

Carmen Rivera
April 28, 2014

ABOUT THE PLAYWRIGHT

Carmen Rivera holds an MA in Playwriting and Latin American Theatre from New York University's Gallatin School. An award-winning playwright, she has written more than 40 plays that have been performed across the United States, Latin America, the Caribbean and Europe.

JULIA DE BURGOS: CHILD OF WATER was first produced at the Puerto Rican Traveling Theatre (PRTT) in 1999 and videotaped for the archives at The Lincoln Center Library for the Performing Arts.

Ms. Rivera's other major works include LA GRINGA, for which she received an OBIE Award in 1996. Since then it has played at Repertorio Español making it Off-Broadway's longest running Spanish language play. LA GRINGA was featured by the Brooklyn Academy of Music as part of their Spanish Voices Series, has played in theatre festivals in Bolivia, Colombia and Puerto Rico, and is published in English and Spanish by Samuel French.

LA LUPE: MY LIFE, MY DESTINY opened Off-Broadway in 2001 and received an ACE Award for Best Production from the Association of Journalists and Writers.

TO CATCH THE LIGHTNING produced at the PRTT in 1997 was also nominated for an ACE Award for Best Production.

Ms. Rivera with Cándido Tirado co-wrote CELIA: THE LIFE AND MUSIC OF CELIA CRUZ, the successful Off-Broadway musical, which received HOLA Awards for Achievement in Playwriting and Best Musical and has toured Miami, Puerto Rico, Chicago and Spain.

Ms. Rivera collaborated with director/choreographer Maria Torres on THE MAGIC OF THE SALSA KINGDOM presented at the Salsa Congress in Southport, England in 2009.

THE NEXT STOP was workshopped at New York Theatre Workshop and produced by INTAR. Repertorio Español produced the play in Spanish as LA PRÓXIMA PARADA.

Ms. Rivera's works have also been presented in other venues such as Teatro Círculo; The Latino Experimental Fantastic Theatre (L.E.F.T. – Founding Member); The Women's Project & Productions; New Georges; La Mama E.T.C.; SOHO Rep; HERE; New Perspectives Theatre; Songs Of Coconut Hill Theatre Festival; Ballet Hispánico (NY); National Public Radio; The Point; La TEA; Theatre for a New City; The Nuyorican Poet's Café; The Henry Street Settlement; The Julia de Burgos Café Teatro; Aaron Davis Hall; Dixon Place; El Puente; City Lights Youth Theatre/Lower East Side Tenement Museum; Theatre 22; UrbanTheater Company (Chicago, Ill.); Raíces Theatre (Buffalo, NY); Taller Puertorriqueño (Philadelphia, PA.); the American Alliance for Theatre and Education Conference; Just Add Water Festival at New York Theatre Workshop and at theatre festivals in Moscow, Chile, Puerto Rico, Colombia and Bolivia.

Ms. Rivera participated at the Lark Playwrights Center -- Mexico/US Exchange program translating plays into English and has been involved in translating LA GRINGA and CELIA: THE LIFE AND MUSIC OF CELIA CRUZ into English and Spanish. She has served as translator (NY Spanish/Spanglish) and as dialect coach for the television show, POWER, produced by Starz.

Ms. Rivera's work is widely anthologized. BETTY'S GARAGE is included in *The Women's Project and Productions: Rowing to America and 16 Other Short Plays*. DELIA'S RACE is included in *Positive/Negative: Women of Color and HIV/ AIDS*, published by Aunt Lute. JULIA is included in *Nuestro*, an anthology of Puerto Rican Theatre published by Penguin USA New York. Ms. Rivera is included in *Women Who Make Theatre* published by Smith and Kraus, and her work can be found in *Alexander Street Press*, an online archive. She is a recipient of grants from the National Endowment for the Arts, ATT On-Stage and New York State Council of the Arts.

Carmen Rivera is a founding member and co-executive director of E.P.P. (Educational Play Productions), which brings plays that deal with social issues into public schools. (www.educationalplayproductions.com)

ABOUT RED SUGARCANE PRESS

RED SUGARCANE PRESS is dedicated to presenting well-known and emerging writers, artists and activists who reflect unique voices and experiences from the grassroots of the Puerto Rican, Caribbean, Latino/a and African diasporas. These works break new ground, educate and entertain as well as challenge and inspire us to embrace new directions toward human liberation.

RED SUGARCANE PRESS is rooted in the journey of indigenous and African peoples in the Americas who from the time of enslavement to the present have struggled for social and economic justice and triumphed through the courage and tenacity of many generations.

Iris Morales
Founder & Publisher

www.redsugarcanepress.com